Unwritten Letters to You

T.B. LABERGE

Edited by Mark Hannah

Cover and interior design
by Christopher Vinca

CONTENTS

To Steve and Judy LaBerge

Your 50 years of marriage have been an example to me. You have taught me that love is something that is worth pursuing and that loving well is not just a feeling, but also a choice that is to be carried out daily.

AUTHOR'S NOTES

In my 25 years of life, I have experienced a multitude of emotions. These pages are the result of those emotions, from the ones who I've lost, to the ones I have loved and still seek to love. It has been a journey that has made me the person I am today. It is a terrible thing to feel such deep things and not be able to let it out, whether that is through music, art or words. To be able to communicate what our hearts most desire to speak is what we all long for. I am so grateful that I have been given this ability to make blood into ink and to make pain into stories. This is the reason for *Unwritten Letters to You*. It is the process of letting go of the past, hoping for the future, and loving the present. Our hearts long for love. In fact, we were created to love, and in the grand romance of life we find that our hearts will often times seek to join in the melody of another's soul.

The words I write, they are the bridge to help connect what our heart wants to say and how our mind can say them. Each word that I have written has come from the deepest parts of longing that I have collected over the years, whether it was the rejection from those that I have loved, or the hope of acceptance for those that I hope to love. Every story, sometimes long, sometimes only a single sentence, all come back to the main story that we are living, and that story is the greatest love story ever; The love that Christ has for you and I.

Nothing will ever show us what love really is besides Jesus Christ, for He laid down His life so that we might join Him in eternal life, so that we may enter His courts with praise and joy. I hope that as you have experienced love in your own life, that you start to see the beauty in Christ's love for you. Because His love is always calling us, always pursuing and inviting us to something better. Love without action is useless, and Christ shows us that His love is active; it always will be.

I truly hope that this book is more than just words, but that you take each section and let it speak to you. This book has been designed so that you can tear out the pages and send them to someone you love, or you can keep it in a spot that is most precious to you. Make this book your own; use it in a way that means something great to you.

I am excited for you to engage with what is said in this book, because I know that we have all felt this on some level, and sharing in this pain and joy is something very special. Thank you for taking the time to read all that I have written, and I hope that it encourages you to write something from the heart, because that is a beautiful place to write from.

-T.B. LaBerge

to the one
I long for

To the one I long for,

I look for you in all the
places I go, and maybe
some day I'll find you.

To the one I long for,

You long for something deep,
and it seems to echo within
the caverns of your soul; like a
haunting song that never ends,
and you are left to dance a
lonely dance.

If I could, I would find my way
to you, hoping to soothe those
pangs of your heart, to make you
remember the soul that you are.

If I could, I would change the song
and let you leave this dance floor.

If I could, I would take your hand,
and walk with you to a place that
was good.

If I could, oh god, if only I could.

To the one I long for,

I can't sing you any song, or paint you a
pretty picture. I can't climb a mountain
or grab the moon. But I can say the things
that have been locked inside my heart;
and I want to say all these unwritten
words that I have kept secret, to you.
Your eyes remind me of all the summers
that broke my heart, and your smile
sings a million untold songs to my soul.
Your happiness makes me happy, and
your sadness makes me sad. You are the
dearest stranger I have ever met, and
I am in desperate need to know you, to
touch you, and to love you. What can I do,
that will make you feel the same? I wish
I was brave enough to say hi, to journey
those miles to you, but I am not; and I fear
I never will be. Maybe, just maybe, this
love I have will make me brave, and we'll
have a journey of our own, to the ends of
the earth and back.

To the one I long for,

It starts with a smile,
or a laugh. Maybe it's
just the way they view
the world. However it
happens, it becomes a
story. I'm still looking
for that smile, that
wink, or maybe it'll
be just a sigh that will
set my world on fire.
Whatever it is, I'm
looking forward to it.

To the one I long for,

I am frightened at the
prospect of how much I might
love you, because I know
the price it brings, and just
thinking of you has begun the
investment process within
my heart. It would be easier
to never invest at all, to hold
all vulnerability close to my
chest, not allowing anyone
to enter my safe. But what a
cruel thing it would be, to deny
an opportunity to love a soul
as beautiful as yours.

To the one I long for,

I'm going to hope, and
hope, and hope, until
one day I do something.
Maybe then, we'll be
able to find that place
that we have both
wanted for so long.
Maybe then, we'll
have each other. I'm
not reaching for stars
anymore. I'm reaching
for you, and honestly,
that's far more
beautiful than a night
full of dancing flames.

To the one I long for,

I am not good with words, but
still my words dance out of chaos,
forming something beautiful. I'm
just hoping that you follow along,
and find your way back to me. I will
write, until you write back. I will
seek, until you look back, and I will
whisper, until you whisper back. I
am always looking for that shadow,
the one that I can never find. I am
always hoping for that hope that I
cannot hold onto. I fear that I love
someone that will always be the
wind to my sails, pushing me on,
but never staying.

To the one I long for,

Maybe one day,
the sad songs won't be
about us. Maybe, we'll
have a happy one.
I hope so, and I'd like to
dance with you to it.

To the one I long for,

I hope that when we
have found that it was
good to be alone, that
we will eventually find
that it is good to be
together; and then we'll
meet and never let go.

To the one I long for,

Love is patient,
and that is the hardest
part of love.

To the one I long for,

If only words could win
hearts over. Because then
I would memorize every
word known to man, and I
would write you a library
worth of books, hoping
to love you with all that I
have learned.

To the one I long for,

The whole world fell
in love with you; but I
hoped that I was the
only one you noticed,
that I somehow I was
the only one you chose.

To the one I long for,

I like to think that
we'll find each other
in a place that is
unfamiliar. But we'll be
okay, because you and
I will find memories
within our smiles; a
lifetime to be had in the
depths of our
dancing eyes.

To the one I long for,

You and I, we could be.
We could be in love,
happy, adventurous, lazy,
driven, overjoyed, sad,
angry, simple, complex,
funny, kissing, together.
We could be, and be and
be and be forever
and always.

To the one I long for,

What if? What if my love and
desire for you broke through
the doubts that cling onto me?
What if I chose to love you even
in the prospect of the unknown?

Would you love me too?

To the one I long for,

What an ache we have
to be loved. What an
ache, what a beautiful,
beautiful ache.

To the one I long for,

I'm sitting here thinking of you, how I
want to be with you. But I don't just want
the idea of you. I want the reality of you;
the you that is hidden to the world. I want
the you without makeup. I want the you
with makeup. I want the you that makes me
angry, I want the you that makes me happy.
I want the you in the cute dress. I want the
you in the sweat pants. I want the you that I
can love well. I want the you that I can be a
friend with. I want the you that I can make
laugh. I want the you that I can make happy.
I want the you that has sad memories, I want
the you that has happy memories. I want the
you that gets happy at seeing a friend. I want
the you that doesn't want to see that one
friend. I want the you from the past, present,
and the future. I want the you whose pillow
has known more tears than dreams. I want
the you whose mind is full of thoughts.

What I am trying to say is that I want you,
all of you.

To the one I long for,

The thing is this;
I can't stop thinking
about you.
Slowly, day by day,
I'm making my way
to you.

To the one I long for,

It was her, when the sun
came up and greeted the
day. It was her when the
moon danced with the
stars. As the world went
to sleep, it was her.

I saw her face when all
the lights had gone out,
and it was her voice that
echoed in the silence.

It was her. And I hoped
that it was me for her.

To the one I long for,

There are days where I can't
think of anything but you. It is
those days that I find it most
difficult to breathe, because you
are not a visitor to my thoughts.
You have become home, the one
person who never leaves the
threshold of my mind, and each
day that I think of you, you
become so deeply rooted within
my soul that I fear if I do not
proclaim my love for you, then
when someone comes along and
you fall in love with them, that
my heart will be uprooted. Is it
meant to be that I linger from
afar? That I simply love you
in silence and pain? Can I not
fly to you, and let these rooted
thoughts grow even more?

To the one I long for,

The music will move and so will
we, and there will be comfort
in the motion of our dance.
Hidden in the moment will be
a promise of a thousand more
slow dances, sometimes in
kitchens late at night, or on a
street corner with a single lamp
illuminating us, or at a friends
wedding. But all the while, it
will be just you and I, dancing
together and feeling our hearts
beat as we hold each other.

Even though the music hasn't
started, and I haven't found my
partner yet, I am learning to
dance while I wait for you.

To the one I long for,

Maybe we will find each
other soon.

To the one I long for,

Do I hold my breath
and pray for rest?
Do I step out and
expect you to be there
when I arrive?
Do I scream into the
night hoping that you
should respond?

Or do I continue on?
Making my way to
a new place; a place
where my rest shall be
real, and my company
pleasant. Where my
screams shall be heard
and my heart shall be
restored.

Shall I leave? Because
I've been waiting; and
it's tearing me apart.

To the one I long for,

I want to love you, love you until it
hurts; until my heart can't handle it,
and my bones seem to ache. I want
to kiss you, hold you, and dance
with you. I want to know how your
soul reacts to a sunrise or a sunset.
I want to be able to guess your first
thoughts, and I want to cherish your
mind like it's the most beautiful place
on earth. I want to laugh with you,
cry with you, and to be with you. You
are magic to me; setting me on fire
but never burning me, destroying me
and yet never hurting me, and I love
you, but I don't know how to say it.

To the one I long for,

And tomorrow is a new day, tomorrow is a day
that I could see your face for the first time,
maybe sit next to you and make a little
small talk.

Tomorrow is an opportunity that I find the
courage to ask you out for a drink, and inquire
what it is that makes you come alive.

Tomorrow could be the day that I find out what
made you who you are, what experience shaped
you into the person that makes my heart beat a
little faster.

Tomorrow might just be the moment that my
hand stops trembling, because I have found a
safe place within the gentle gaze of your eyes.

Tomorrow could be the place where I hold your
hand, feeling the next 60 years being born in
between the folds of our hands.

Tomorrow, what a brilliant thought it is, to
know that you might be hidden within that day,
just waiting to say hello and starting this grand
adventure with me.

Tomorrow, what a wonderful place it is, where
I could have a single second to say something,
that would start a million moments with
someone, who makes every moment feel as
though I am outside of time altogether.

To the one I long for,

If you knew how much
I thought of you, would
you run from me? or fall
in love with me? It's as
if I am torn between the
thoughts of having you
and the thoughts of losing
you. They both terrify
me, for I know that I am
not good enough, but I am
striving to be. All I ask
is for patience, so that I
may one day wake up and
make the right choice; the
choice of loving you well.

to the One
I Lost

To the one I lost,

You wrote so much into my story, and I find myself re-reading the words you left. They are beginning to fade, and I'm wondering how this next chapter is going to sound without your voice in it.

To the one I lost,

I'm sorry for saying words
that were said before they
should have been. I'm sorry
for enforcing thoughts of a
future, when I should have been
focusing on the present. I'm
sorry for making you more than
who you are, when I should
have been guarding a heart that
is fragile. I'm sorry for being
the wrong person and thinking
I was the right one. I'm sorry
I created a home inside my
mind, when in reality I moved
on. I'm sorry for the pain, when
I should have brought a smile.
I'm sorry for it all, because you
didn't deserve it at all.

To the one I lost,

My pain once
mattered to you.

To the one I lost,

I am running out of
words. My thoughts have
gone from vocabulary
to touch, from touch to
wishes, from wishes to
sighs. Now my very lungs
have begun to empty,
and I fear that I shall
be nothing more than a
memory to you.

To the one I lost,

She reminded me of
sadness, happiness,
and all the seasons of
the heart.

To the one I lost,

I suffer from the
thought that you might
fit better within the
arms of another.

To the one I lost,

I wanted to be a forever,
but I was only a moment.

To the one I lost,

You were so sad, and I
wanted to wipe away
your tears. But so was I,
and I couldn't even wipe
away my own tears.

To the one I lost,

I wanted you to know that I thought
about you today. Like the rippling of
a lake after a rock has been thrown
in, you seem to reverberate every
inch of me. It's so odd how something
so small can affect something so big.
And yet, here you are affecting me
from so far away. I wish these tiny
little waves never stopped, but one
day they will and all will be smooth
and calm again. It terrifies me to
think about that day, to think of a
world without thinking about you.

to the One I Love

To the one I love,

To have but one life to share,
and to invest in you, that
noblest of treasures; the love
that pushes you closer to that
greatest Love, that love which
would say unto Christ "I have
invested what You have given,
so that this treasure would
not be mine, but Yours forever
more." and that is all that I
ever hope to do, to give you
unto Christ, just as He has
given you unto me.

To the one I love,

You were alive before they came around, so don't let them stop you from living again. Just because they didn't want you doesn't mean you are unwanted. Just because they didn't want forever with you doesn't mean you don't deserve a forever. Just because love wasn't written for you both doesn't mean your life is written with any less love.

You are going to breathe again, because they might have taken the breath from you, but they can't take the rest of you.

To the one I love,

Help me love you, won't
you darling? For I am a
simple man, always in
need of a gentle hand and
a heart of patience. Let
me learn what it means
to soothe your pain, and
what it is that you seek
at the end of the day;
because I'm trying, and
I'll always be wanting to
love you more.

To the one I love,

Let's dance, and leave the worries
to rest. Let us examine what our
hearts have always wanted, and
discuss what tomorrow may bring.
Maybe we could just walk for a little
bit and find ourselves under the
stars, loving only that moment, and
not thinking about the past hurts.
I should hope to begin again with
you, and find that my weariness
in the struggle of searching for
love has vanished. Because here
you are, looking and choosing, and
holding fast to the words we speak.
Speak steady and true, for my soul
is seeking to write them down and
engrave them in the most
precious places.

To the one I love,

Maybe we could love
each other a little bit
now, and then we can
love each other a lot
later. Then we can just
eventually love always.

To the one I love,

I don't know why, but
I think the moon has
been saying your name
to me at night, because
you stumble into my
dreams more often
than usual.

To the one I love,

Who stole your smile?
Who robbed you of your laugh?
Just because they made you
feel alive once, does not mean
they are allowed to make you
feel like death. Reclaim the
smile you once loved, and take
back that beautiful laughter
that makes you feel the depths
of life once again. You are more
than the marks that have been
left on your soul, more than
the tears of a broken heart;
you are a soul that is eternal.

To the one I love,

There was enough of
you in my heart to fill
the world; and still,
I wanted more.

To the one I love,

Perhaps we'll find a
place where we're both
ready; perhaps we're
both lost and we haven't
found the map to that
land. But maybe, just
maybe, we'll find our
way there one day.

To the one I love,

I think you had the fire of the
stars within you; because even
though you are not with me, I
still see your glow from afar.

Maybe I'll make a wish and
you'll come back to me.
Then I can find my favorite
constellation in your eyes, and
kiss you until the stars sleep.

To the one I love,

You must not reduce
yourself to a puddle just
because the person you
like is afraid to swim and
you are a fierce sea to
them. Because there will
be someone who was born
with love of the waves
within their blood, and
they will look at you with
fear and respect.

To the one I love,

We once learned to
breathe, eat, walk, laugh,
love, and live. Now we're
learning to heal.

To the one I love,

I can't speak! I can't think!
I can't breathe! How am I to
let you know that I love you,
when just looking at you takes
all of me?

I could love you from here, I
could love you from there, and
I think I could love you
from anywhere.

To the one I love,

When it comes to love,
I think we meet in a
place of uncertainty,
and then we make our
way from there, until
we have found our
way home.

To the one I love,

You work so hard, just
to end up at home
crying yourself to sleep.
Remember you're
trying, you are moving
mountains that have
plagued you since you
were young, and you're
trying so hard.

Keep fighting; fight
until you have won;
fight until you have
found your way home,
until the sun comes
back and your heart
learns to love the
mornings again.

To the one I love,

I could read the history
of her life in the depths
of her eyes; I learned
then that history was
my favorite subject.

To the one I love,

You wear strength so
well, I forget that you
have to take it off at
the end of the day, still
feeling the marks that
it leaves on your soul.

To the one I love,

You mean more to me
than my words can express.
Your value outweighs my
vocabulary. No melody of
thought can adequately
explain the soul that you
are. The beauty that resides
within you outshines the
expanse of my mind. It
hurts, because I want to tell
you this; but I find myself
stuck in the void of past
mistakes.

To the one I love,

All this noise for so long; I
just want to hear your voice,
telling me that you love me
and that we'll be together.

I think that even the stars
loved you; because they were
the ones who gazed upon you
each night, and your beauty
made them dance across
the sky.

To the one I love,

What is heartbreak?
It's when you thought you
had forever on the clock,
and the other person
decided to stop time.
It's everything, and then
nothing; a cold hand, and
silence on the other end of
the phone. Wanting to say
good morning, but instead
having to greet the day,
and everyday, with no one
around. It's the knot in the
back of your throat, the
warmth and stickiness that
a tear leaves on your cheek;
But in the end, it's growth,
and weakness learning to
be strong.

To the one I love,

How wonderful;
this world with you in it.

To the one I love,

It's as though my mind
has made a home for
you, my soul has set a
place at the table and
my heart is calling your
name over and over
again; I hope that you
accept the invitation
to stay.

To the one I love,

You felt all the love in
the world, and for that,
you received all the
pain that comes with it.
Yet, you still loved, and
for that you are seen
as beautiful.

To the one I love,

Let me plant
future promises
in the garden
of your soul,
so that we
might live together
in the fruits
of our labor.

To the one I love,

And I thought,
here is the woman
I want to make smile
until death do us part.

To the one I love,

I have spent far too
many days thinking of
you, when I should have
been talking with you.

To the one I love,

Listen to the battered
hearts; for they have
survived to tell the
tales of love.

To the one I love,

If my hands were full
or if they were empty,
would you accept them?
Because I am offering
them no matter what
they hold; for your hands
are all I want in mine.

To the one I love,

My love for you is one
born in hope; I wish
not that it end in fear.

To the one I love,

If I must lose myself in order
to be found with you, then let
it be known that I am lost and
I hope to never be found.

To the one I love,

Who hurt you?

Who would touch the
stars, and burn them?

Who would kiss the
waves, and drown
them?

Who would climb the
mountains, and bury
them?

Who would hurt you?
Oh love, who hurt you?

To the one I love,

You create beautiful
chaos within my soul;
and I don't know what
to do with it, other than
stare and be amazed.

To the one I love,

Love is saying I do;
even when you feel like
you don't.

To the one I love,

I want to kiss you until we
both forget the reason why
we started kissing in the first
place. I want to hold you until
our breathing is synchronized,
like the waves of the ocean. I
want to brush your hair out of
your eyes and tell you that they
are the most beautiful things I
have ever seen. I want to laugh
with you until we cry, because
those are the only tears that I
want you to ever have. I want all
these moments to be with you;
for now and forever.

To the one love,

It's there; a sadness that lays
at the center of your heart,
keeping you company when
the world has left you alone.
I don't know what to say, but
sometimes tears fall and you
can't do anything but live
with it. I know, though, that
one day you will no longer
have that. It will be but a
memory. Please hold on. You
won't hurt forever. You'll love
and laugh again. Just stay
strong until you have felt the
sun on your face, and you
know that you have made it...
Just hold on. The pain will be
silenced one day.

To the one I love,

And I hope, as I often do,
that you are waiting there;
at the end of the day.

To the one I love,

If I have but one life, let me
spend it beside yours; living
each moment as though I
have invested it wisely.

To the one I love,

I want to decorate your
heart with the promise
of love.

To the one I love,

You feel it most when it all goes silent; the small groan of a lonely heart. And it whispers to you, reminding you that you miss the heartbeat of someone you have not met. You start to realize how much you want it, how it has become something more than a longing, but rather, a deep and cruel pain that refuses to let go.

Then you breathe in deeply, and you live. Because life is not found in tomorrow, but in every beat of your own heart. This is how you keep that lonely heart at bay, by being, and being, and being until all becomes calm again. Your roots do not dig into the soil of empty promises, but in the depths of present reality. So grow, and grow, and grow, until spring has bloomed and the world is full of life again.

To the one I love,

You deserve more than
a borrowed heart.

To the one I love,

And all the mornings we could have
together spent talking, eating, laughing,
snoozing a little longer and just enjoying
each other; I want all these things.

I want those mornings where we both
don't know what's going on, the sleep still
clinging to our very bodies, begging for us
to return to our beds. I want those days
where you kiss me awake, and I see your
puffy face smiling back at me. I want to
brush aside the hair that has fallen down
your beautifully worn face. I want to kiss
you until we remember that we are late for
work. I want to hold you until it is noon,
and we have wasted all the hours of our
day; but it will be time well invested.

To the one I love,

I want these things, those
moments of living life, where
it was once silent and alone;
is now spent with another
soul next to me.

I want them; and I want
them with you.

To the one I love,

May I be but one thought in your head?
May I be but one single moment of
complete bliss to you?

I should hope that the thought of me
should make you smile, because each
second that I ponder your heart I am
set ablaze.

To the one I love,

You'll find that as you grow older you start to realize that age brings sadness. But it also brings opportunities for happiness. You'll have days when it seems like you are alone, and that will make you sad; but there will be days when the silence reminds you of something that will make you smile. Breathe, live, and love. This is life; this is the process of growing up.

To the one I love,

I want to grow old and
comfortable with you.

To the one I love,

My love for you is not poetry; it is
late nights of agonizing thoughts
and long days of selfless actions. It
weighs upon my mind like a mad
riddle. As I grow older, it becomes
more obvious how hard it is to love
selflessly; how much responsibility
it holds.

If I am to love you at all, it is only
through the grace of Christ. For I
am not enough, but I know He is.

To the one I love,

If you are happy, then I am happy. If you are sad, then I am sad. Because it's not about whether or not I fix you, it's about me being here and sharing the weight of these moments with you. I fight beside you, because that is love. It's sharing the struggles, the joys and love we have. It's about walking this life together, and I want you there for as long as possible.

You are dear to me, and greatly adored. You are held in the most precious place of my heart; and I hope you remain there.

To the one I love,

Come walk with me. I
like your company and
I've been alone for so
long. Your laugh will
be a pleasant reminder
that there is beauty in
this world.

To the one I love,

I'm angry, I'm angry with the boy who said he would love you till the day he died, but I guess he died when he left you. I'm angry at the boy who made you think your innocence could so easily be taken when it was never his to take. I'm angry that he made you vulnerable, and now you regret ever being so open. I'm angry, because he was a lesson you never signed up for, and we were never meant to learn from the class of heartbreak. I'm angry, and I can't do anything about it but say that you're worth more than what he gave or took; you're worth more than late nights full of tears and early mornings filled with silence.

You are the warmth in a hug, and the beauty in a sunrise; and I'm sorry that he made you feel like the cold in an empty room and the smoke of a blown out candle. I can only hope that you'll love yourself again, because a star may feel alone and unwanted, but the world lays in wonder of the beauty that star gives. Your soul is endless; it would be a shame to think anyone could steal that truth.

You will hear a song, and it will rest in the back of your throat, making a knot that will hold fast. You'll feel the hot streaks of tears coming down your face, reminding you of a moment in time when you were in love. The crisp autumn air filling your lungs, the joy of endless possibilities that occupied your thoughts and heart; it all comes crashing down again, as you listen to the melody of a song that once meant something wonderful. It hurts, but you repeat it again and again, hoping that it becomes a happy tune to you once more; because you loved that song, and you don't want to lose that as well.

To the one I love,

I'm glad your last boyfriend had such a short
vocabulary, because I've been studying how to
describe beauty for my whole life, been training
myself to serve and love. I've been constructing
myself to show you the true value that you
hold, that I think stars are made from your
smile, that the sun rises just so we can
be together.

I'm glad your boyfriend didn't have the courage
that I do; that I'd fight the years to be with you,
knowing that it will end with me growing old by
your side.

I'm glad your boyfriend didn't see you through
the same lens I do, for you are 20/20 and it's
getting stronger everyday.

But I'm sad, because you had to have a
boyfriend who didn't love you like you should
be loved. Because to me, you're not just a pretty
little flower, You're the whole world in spring,
and I'm in love with this season.

To the one I love,

The pain of missing
someone always starts
in the chest, where the
heart is. Then it makes its
way toward the gut. This
is when you become aware
of how lost you are without
this person, and then one
day it disappears. That is
the weirdest feeling of all.

To the one I love,

I know that you can be
strong without being happy,
that you can press on
without having a smile, but
oh darling, I would love to
make you happy and to help
make you smile. If only for a
moment, to be able to clear
those storm clouds, and
bring a little sunshine into
your life.

To the one I love,

You're a slow dance
waiting to happen.

To the one I love,

Yes, it hurts now. But
remember that you'll laugh
again; that rainbows appear
when storms have passed,
and that our joy comes in
the morning. Maybe you just
need to rest and let your
heart heal. When you have
cried all that you can cry
and your tears have dried
you'll feel a stillness to it all.
Then you'll get up and make
yourself a cup of tea, and
the sun will shine on you as
you close your eyes. Learn to
breathe in deeply, then feel
the beat of your heart, and
know that you are not really
broken; that one day you too
can know what it means to
love without loss.

To the one I love,

I felt it all, I still feel it,
and I wonder if I will
continue to feel it.

.

To the one I love,

Oh you were beautiful,
when your hair was a mess
and your face a wreck.
You were beautiful when you
slept and when you wept.
You were beautiful when
you never thought you were,
because I saw you in those
moments. I saw all of you;
and oh how I loved you.

To the one I love,

You feel like a stranger
in a foreign land without
their love, don't you?
Just remember that this
world once felt foreign,
but you learned to live;
and you'll learn to
love again.

To the one I love,

Would you stay and talk to me? Just until this storm has passed; because your voice soothes the waves that have been crashing against my soul, and I'm so tired.

Be here with me, and let's talk of love, hope, peace and the joys of tomorrow; it's so dark and the world is so hurt, but if we talk for a little while, maybe we can bring a little light to where we are.

So, stay with me, and let's talk until the pounding has stopped, and the world is silent and still again.

To the one I love,

I swear flowers grow where your
heart is; because it is always
spring when you are near. I hope
that my words are not just that,
but that I have the courage to show
love with each day that passes.
You deserve someone who will help
you grow those flowers, instead of
just admiring them.

to the one
who loves

To the one who loves,

You will love being single, you will love not having to talk to anyone or do anything for a day, that you can do whatever you want because you are the master of your own life. But one day, you will realize that you want to be unselfish for someone; that you would rather have a lifetime with another soul than without; and that desire of being "free" that you so long held dear will become a prison. Loving someone will start to be a freedom for you, and you will break all the chains of solitude that you once loved, just so you can experience the breathing process of loving another; this is when you know, that something within you has changed, and that you will never be the same.

I'm tired of looking forward. I am standing in this moment so that my past will be proud and my future will be grateful. We have only today; let's learn to love it.

To the one who loves,

One day it's 12:27 am, and you're sad. Not because of how life is treating you or anything. It's just because you want someone next to you. Someone, who at the end of the day, will look at you and smile, asking what you want to have for dinner. You'll realize that you are longing for love, a comfortable and simple love; one that gives you a reason to shut off the computer and just have a conversation. You want a companion who will be there, who will be willing to give you space and who will also keep you close. It's hard, because as you think, the clock slowly turns to 12:30am, and you are just tired of trying, and you just want it to happen. But it will, and you'll look back at these late nights, and smile; wishing you could tell your single self that it's going to be okay, that all the "No's" were leading you to a beautiful yes. So, as it gets later, you just need to remember that your sadness will be replaced with an overwhelming gratitude that you are loved; and that will be better than all the missed opportunities and made up dreams that you had.

To the one who loves,

And who cares for you? The one who is so caring? Who lets you know that it's going to be okay, and that you are allowed to be weak? Who tells you to be kind to yourself and to know that love is to be received as well? Who cares for you? Who do you allow into your well crafted life that you have kept so close? Who have you allowed to walk in that most precious place that you call your soul? I hope whoever it is, enters with the intention of making it a home, and caring for it. Be careful, you who care so much, because you still need to be cared for as well.

To the one who loves,

No one has been brave enough
to love you, and that shouldn't
make you sad. Because you'll
find someone who fears you but
is still brave enough to be with
you, and that is worth a little
heartbreak for now.

Love will come, and it will
need a courageous soul to stand
and fight with.

To the one who loves,

You think "One day" this and
"one day" that, but you need
to focus on this day; because
just maybe, that one day
will be today.

To the one who loves,

Does she scare you a little?
Good. She should make you
fear her love, so that when
she lets you be apart of it,
you won't take it lightly.
She should remind you
of the power that beauty
brings, that storms reside
in her veins, and that
she still wants you in the
middle of it all. Do not take
this soul for granted, for
she is fierce, and she can
take you places that you
never thought you could
go. But she is still loving in
the midst of it all. Like the
calm rain after a storm, she
can bring life. Learn her,
cherish her, respect her,
and love her; for she is so
much more than a pretty
face, she is a soul on fire.

To the ones who write,

You have just finished the book, and
now you are left with blank pages.
But why? So that you can add your
own stories, because we all deserve to
make an effort in expressing what is
on our hearts. I want you to go boldly
into that unknown place, where love
is wonderful and worth striving for.
Now is the time to find the words that
your heart has always wanted to spill
out, and now is the time for you to
make what was once empty now full.
You have so much to say, and I want
you to add it to this book and be a part
of this journey with me. I hope upon
hope that you find the courage to write
what you truly feel compelled to write,
so that you may enrich this book even
more! Take time with everything you
want to say. There is no rush, and I'm
sure whatever you write will be great,
because if it comes from the heart of
someone who truly wants to discover
love, then that is a good thing indeed.

-T.B. LaBerge

ABOUT THE AUTHOR

Todd Benjamin Pierson LaBerge was born to Steve and Judy LaBerge in Illinois on, May 4th 1989. He is the youngest of four boys, and he has loved reading from an early age due to his home-schooled upbringing. He discovered his love for writing when he joined Tumblr in 2011. There, he quickly began writing what was on his heart and through doing so, he gained a following. He currently lives in Georgia where he continues to write and make films at *Brand RED Studios*.

Tumblr: *tblaberge.tumblr.com*
Facebook: *ToddLaBerge1989*
Instagram: *tblaberge*
Twitter: *@tblaberge*
Vimeo: *toddlaberge*